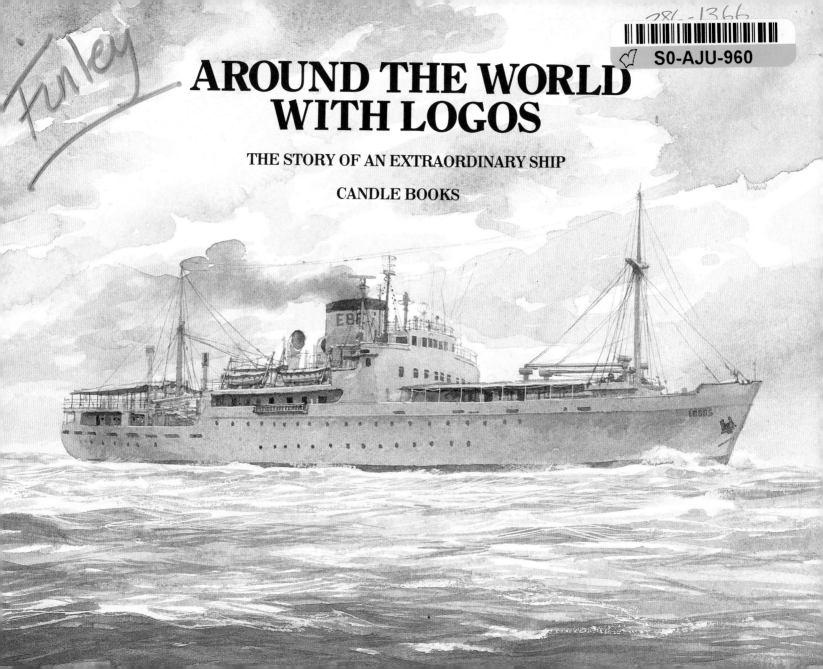

AROUND THE WORLD WITH LOGOS

THE STORY OF AN EXTRAORDINARY SHIP

CANDLE BOOKS

Once upon a time...
No – that's not right. This isn't a made-up story –
although sometimes you'd hardly believe it. Everything
in this story really happened in real places to real people.

This is the story of a ship. A very special ship.
But even before the ship, there was a crew. Captain Bjorn
from Norway; John, the Chief Engineer, from Australia;
Alfred the cook, from Germany; Rashad, an officer from
the Middle East; and Dave, an English engineer.
A crew which came from all over the world – but no
ship! Bjorn, John, Rashad, Alfred, Dave and the others
believed God wanted them to sail round the world taking
Bibles and good books to people everywhere. But first
they had to find their ship!

The crew searched everywhere for a ship. They visited shipyards, met shipowners, rang up scrap yards and asked friends. They kept on praying: 'Lord, help us find our ship!'

Then at last they found it! She was a Danish ship, called the *Umanak*. She was built to sail in the icy waters round Greenland, though experts said she could be altered to sail in hot climates too. So they decided to buy her.

But the crew didn't yet have all the money needed; they still had to raise £25,000! What could they do? They prayed again: 'Lord, help us find the money we need to buy the ship.'

The crew's prayers were answered. Many people all over the world – from young children to old people – sent gifts to help buy the ship. Just one month later, when the time came to pay the ship's owner, the crew found they had all the money they required! How they all enjoyed the special ice-cream cake they had bought to celebrate!

Once the crew from all over the world had bought their ship, there was plenty of work to do.

'First let's give the *Umanak* a new name,' said someone. 'That'll show she has a new job to do.'

'I know!' said a second. 'Let's call her the *Jolly Roger*!'

They all laughed.

Then someone else said: 'Let's call her the *Logos*. That's a Greek word that the Bible uses to talk about Jesus Christ – and we're going to tell thousands of people in many countries about his love.'

So they painted the name *Logos* boldly on the ship's hull.

But the rest of the ship was in a sad state; she'd been allowed to get terribly rusty and dirty. The crew set to work immediately, cleaning out the cabins and passageways, repairing, painting and polishing. The ship's kitchen – called the 'galley' – was particularly messy. Imagine the smells in there before it was made clean and tidy!

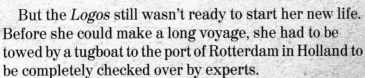

But the *Logos* still wasn't ready to start her new life. Before she could make a long voyage, she had to be towed by a tugboat to the port of Rotterdam in Holland to be completely checked over by experts.

She hadn't been long at sea before the towing-cable to the tug snapped. A brave sailor climbed up a swaying rope-ladder from the tugboat to the slippery deck of the *Logos* and helped link the two ships together again. The towing cable snapped several more times before they were moored safely in Rotterdam harbour.

Now the *Logos* had to be prepared to sail the world's oceans. The main engines were made ready for the heavy work ahead. A huge propellor was fitted to drive the ship through angry waves. Workmen checked that the ship wouldn't let in water. Engineers made the ship ready to sail in hot weather.

At last, after three months' hard work, the *Logos* was ready to begin her task visiting the world's ports, great and small.

We already know that the *Logos* was an unusual ship. Its crew came from all over the world to do the special job of taking good books to people in many different countries. Most ships just have sailors on board. But the *Logos* was different; the crew of the *Logos* brought their families too.

So, from the very first voyage, there were lots of children on board. The children were lucky because they had their own floating school room and travelling teachers. From the *Logos* they could see many exciting things – dolphins, flying fish and sometimes even a passing whale!

Often when the ship docked in a new port the teachers arranged special visits for the children. In the Philippines they visited a pineapple canning factory. In Sri Lanka they visited a place where trees are grown to give rubber. And best of all, in Singapore the children visited a crocodile farm!

The *Logos* arrived in the hot country of Bangladesh soon after a terrible war had ended. While the *Logos* was at anchor there, a terrifying storm arose, tearing the canvas covers off her lifeboats.

Suddenly a look-out shouted: 'Look! There's a man in the water.'

Sure enough, a bobbing figure was being carried at great speed down the fast-moving river, with his capsized boat beneath him.

'We must try to save him,' said the look-out.

'No, no – in this storm it's simply too dangerous,' the captain said firmly. 'The rescue boat would be swept away too.'

No sooner had he said this, than the storm died away as suddenly as it had begun.

'Launch the boat!' ordered the captain. 'Now we can go to the rescue.'

Quickly sailors lowered a motor boat, jumped into it, and steered down river. Soon they were pulling the drowning man out of the water. They sailed back to the *Logos,* helped the man aboard, dried him thoroughly and put him to bed. As soon as the ship's doctor said the rescued man was well enough, they took him back to his village.

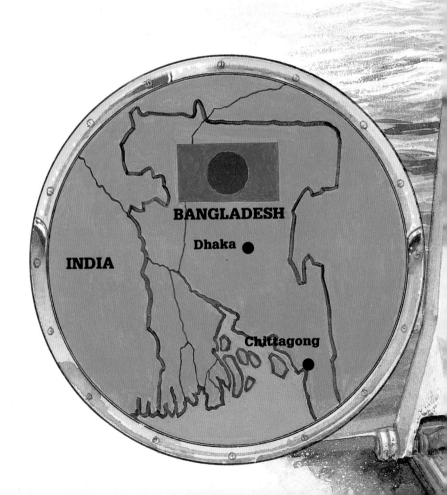

The *Logos* also visited the colourful port of Saigon, the capital of South Vietnam, where another terrible war was coming to an end. Many soldiers patrolled the bombed and battered streets. On the first day in Saigon, so many excited visitors wanted to visit the ship that some of them climbed across steel girders to get on board.

While they were in Vietnam, the crew of the *Logos* held many meetings – for doctors, for business people, for women, for young people, for school children and many others. They explained to their visitors about life on board ship – and told them the good news about what Jesus had done for a suffering world.

Sometimes they showed Christian films, using the side of the ship as a screen. And, as usual, they opened the book exhibition and sold hundreds of Bibles and other books to both young and old. The day before they left, some women from the city came aboard the ship and showed their thanks by cooking a delicious meal of rice and vegetables for everybody on board ship. How do you think the children on board enjoyed that?

Later, the *Logos* was sailing in the South China Sea, when the look-out suddenly noticed something odd. He frowned and looked more carefully through his binoculars.

'It's a tiny fishing-boat, absolutely crowded with people,' he said. 'They must be "boat-people" from Vietnam, trying to escape the war in their country.'

'We must help them,' answered the captain. But he had to be very cautious. 'Sometimes boats like this are full of pirates in disguise,' he explained. 'If we let them on board they might turn on us and take over our ship.'

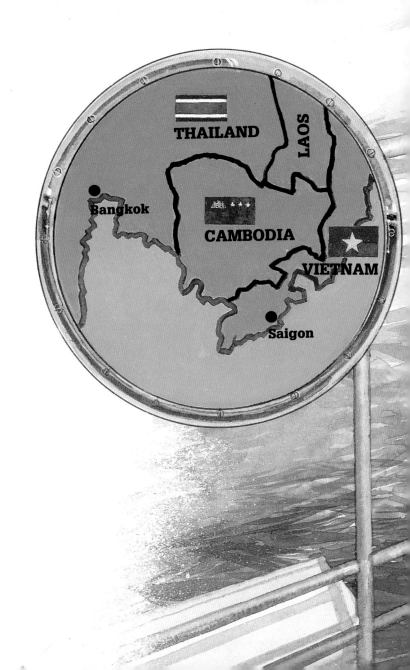

The crew of the *Logos* prayed to God to show them the right thing to do. Then they sailed their big ship alongside the little fishing boat. The boat-people climbed wearily up the ship's ladder to the deck of the *Logos*, many of them crying for joy. There were fifty-three of them altogether, including seven children, and they had been at sea many days. They were washed and given clean clothes, and then examined by the ship's doctor. Finally they were given a hot meal and somewhere to sleep.

For eight weeks the boat-people lived on board the *Logos,* and they became close friends of the crew. Then, when the ship sailed into Bangkok, the capital of friendly Thailand, the visitors were taken to a special camp, while arrangements were made for them to settle in Britain. There many of the Vietnamese boat-people set up home and began a new life.

In January 1988 the *Logos* was leaving the port of Ushuaia in Argentina to sail through the Beagle Channel, at the southernmost tip of South America. Sailors fear this as one of the most dangerous seas in the world. At certain times of year, wild winds rage through the channel.

The captain was tired and went to get some sleep. A busy night lay ahead. He was woken by his ship's phone. It was the pilot, who had come on board to steer the *Logos* through the narrow channel.

'I want to leave the ship,' said the pilot.

'But we're not through the channel yet.'

'It's quite easy now,' the pilot said.

The captain thought hard. Then he said: 'All right. You can go!'

But in those rough seas, it wasn't easy for the pilot to get safely into his own boat, as it rose and fell on the huge waves.

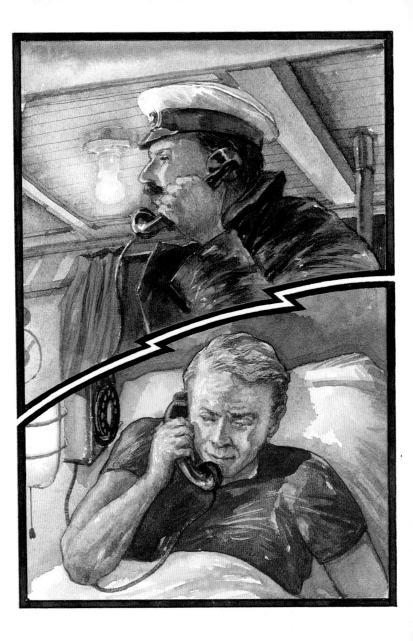

Once the pilot had gone, the captain swung the *Logos* round to steer out of the narrow channel.

'That's odd,' he thought. 'We don't seem to be moving at all!'

He looked at his dials to check that the engine was still running. Yes! It was.

The worried captain realised that the ship must have become caught in a powerful and dangerous current.

Crrrrashhh! Crrash!

The ship had gone aground.

'Stop the engines!' shouted the captain. 'Everyone must put on life-jackets!'

The engineer rushed down many stairways and ladders to the very bottom of the ship. He had to inspect the damage. No – the engines weren't broken. But suddenly he noticed that the hull was badly bent and buckled. He realised that the ship was stuck fast on rocks hidden beneath the wild sea.

The radio officer radioed SOS for help, and soon a navy boat from nearby Chile was racing alongside the *Logos*. The Chilean captain knew these waters well. Together the two captains tried to shift the *Logos* off the rocks. She kept rocking from side to side, so the captain of the *Logos* ordered the engines full-ahead to try to tear her off.

Everyone on board, adults and children, prayed: 'Lord, help us!'

The engineer went below again. Suddenly he heard what he most feared.

He called the captain: 'Water is pouring in. The ship is holed, and filling with water fast.'

'We must abandon ship,' decided the captain. 'Prepare the lifeboats!'

By now the *Logos* was tilted over, making it very difficult to lower the lifeboats. On one side of the ship the boats swung out over the sea; on the other side they banged against her hull. But nobody panicked. Each person quietly took their turn to get into a swaying lifeboat. There was no room for luggage, and the children had to leave behind their favourite toys and games. When the boats were full, they were lowered carefully into the angry sea. Last to go was the lifeboat containing the captain.

Soon all six lifeboats were safely afloat in the swirling water. Two lifeboats had engines and towed the rest, and within half an hour everybody was safe aboard the ships that had come to the rescue of the *Logos*. All 139 people aboard the *Logos* were saved; no one was lost, or even badly hurt.

As the lifeboats were sailing away from the *Logos*, a great rainbow arched into the sky, reminding everyone of the rainbow that Noah saw after the Flood.

But this wasn't the end of the story. Although the *Logos* was lost, her task wasn't completed. So the crew and their friends started to pray: 'Lord, give us another ship.'

In October 1988 they found the right ship to replace *Logos*. She was a Greek ship, called the *Argo* – but she was soon renamed *Logos II*. Her story will be just as exciting as the story of *Logos*!

Facts and figures about the *Logos*

The *Logos* sailed 231,250 sea miles.
The *Logos* visited 258 ports.
The *Logos* visited 103 countries.
7,480,000 people visited the *Logos.*
51,000,000 books and leaflets were sold or given away.
450,000 Bibles and New Testaments were sold or given away.

The *Logos* was built in 1949 in Denmark.
2319 tons
82 metres long
13.4 metres wide
144 passengers and crew

Maybe one day you will be able to visit *Logos II*, the new ship.

Or perhaps you would like to write to some of the children living on board.

You can find out more about *Logos II* by writing to:

Logos II, Postfach 1565, D-6950 Mosbach, Germany.